THE AGE OF GLAMOUR
An Art Deco Coloring Book

The Age of Glamour: An Art Deco Coloring Book
© 2017 Victoria and Albert Museum/Thames & Hudson

Text and V&A images © 2017 Victoria and Albert Museum
Line illustrations and layout © 2017 Thames & Hudson

Line illustrations by Emilia Buggins

First published in the United States of America in 2017 by Thames & Hudson
in association with the Victoria and Albert Museum.

www.thamesandhudsonusa.com

ISBN 978-0-500-42069-0

Printed and bound in China by C & C Offset Printing Co. Ltd

V&A Publishing
Supporting the world's leading
museum of art and design,
the Victoria and Albert
Museum, London

THE AGE OF GLAMOUR
An Art Deco Coloring Book

Thames & Hudson | V&A

INTRODUCTION

'As for reality we like it exotic'

Theatre review by G. Bauer,
Annales, 18 October 1925

THE TERM ART DECO covers a period of great innovation in design, beginning in the early 20th century and peaking in the 1920s and 1930s. The huge variety of designs that appeared in this period cannot be reduced to one easily captured 'look'. They range from the controlled curves of glassware by René Lalique, to the dynamic geometry of the Chrysler Building in New York. But there are recurring elements that unite Art Deco designs, or, as one contemporary observer put it, give them a 'family resemblance' to each other.

Art Deco is uncluttered and elegant. It is characterized by smooth lines, geometric shapes, two-dimensional ornament, and a taste for symmetrical and streamlined forms. These simple, stylized shapes took over from the lavish ornamentation that proliferated on ceramics, dress and furnishings in the Victorian era, and the sinuous naturalism of Art Nouveau. Bright colour contrasts kept Art Deco designs vivid and fresh. Its visual language, informed by industrial design, immediately says 'modernity'. Art Deco was celebrated as the most fashionable style of the modern age at the 1925 Paris *Exposition Internationale des Arts*

Décoratifs et Industriels Modernes. It then swept across the globe, from Japan to India and South America, on a wave of popularity. The term 'Art Deco' was coined only in the 1960s (a decade equally keen to situate itself at the cutting-edge). Prior to this, the style was known by names including 'Zig-Zag modern', 'Jazz modern' and simply 'Moderne'.

Despite its simplicity of line, Art Deco manages to be playful and romantic. This was the fabled 'Jazz Age' in America and a time of fantasy and exoticism. 'Every aspect of modern living was given an exotic veneer,' writes curator Ghislaine Wood, 'from the façades of factories and cinemas to the packaging of perfumes and chocolates. The ubiquitous iconography of tropical birds and animals, lush vegetation, sunbursts, dancing girls, lotuses, ogees and zigzags gave an exotic flourish to all kinds of design.'[1] Increased travel during this period brought many new design influences and ideas into circulation, but Hollywood films offered an even more popular window onto distant lands. Featuring spectacular and often wildly romanticized settings, they ensured the spread of its influence to a wide audience, being seen by

NOTES
1. Ghislaine Wood, 'The Exotic' *Art Deco* 1910–39, 2003, p.125.

Art Deco iconography, including the graphic sunburst motif, has had a lasting influence, as seen in this strong repeat pattern by Lucienne Day from the 1960s (right).

an estimated 80 million people a week by the mid-1930s. Art Deco fashion plates depicted filmic scenes, elegantly framed, within exotic landscapes and interiors. Idealized figures in draped clothing wander among snow-laden Japanese cherry trees perhaps, recline with a cigarette on Chinese cushions, or dance on a moonlit terrace.

The deep blacks and silhouettes of Art Deco design also reflect the language of film. Designers set these off with strong, cool colours — steel blue, orange, grey, green, white — a departure from the warmer and more muted colours of Art Nouveau. The bold use of colour and line in Art Deco also reflects the gradual popularization of radical aesthetics introduced by earlier avante-garde art movements. The influence of Cubism, the movement generally agreed to have begun around 1907 with Pablo Picasso's famous painting *Les Demoiselles d'Avignon*, is evident in Art Deco's strong geometric lines. The colour palette of the period pays tribute to the strong colours and fierce brushwork of early 20th-century Fauvists such as Henri Matisse.

Designers also looked back for inspiration from history and the Classical and ancient past. New archaeological finds sparked new ideas. The discovery of the tomb of the Egyptian boy-king Tutankhamun in November 1922 started a craze known as 'Tutmania' in Europe and America. Everything from jewellery and bags to furniture, cinema façades and book bindings took on an Egyptian flavour. Other traditions, such as the bourgeois Louis-Philippe styles of early 19th-century France, were mined for inspiration and modernized in the search for the new. Natural forms of flowers and foliage remained ever-present, particularly on textiles, but were shaped to fit the stylized lines of modernity.

Art Deco was at first a luxury style, characterized by the grand décor of new ocean liners such as the SS *Normandie*, or sophisticated restaurants such as the China Tang in The Dorchester, London. It became associated with leisure, pleasure, glamour and fun. Interior designers employed expensive materials including silver, crystal, ivory, jade and lacquer, which reflected the light and added to the sparkle of their settings. The glamour of 1920s Art Deco seemed all the greater as a relief from the austere war years that preceded it in Europe.

The 1930s, by contrast, were a decade in which Art Deco became more than a movement for the elite and reached out to a whole new audience. Cheaper materials such as chrome and plastics, and industrial manufacturing catered to a growing market for elegant and functional designs. Alongside the romantic and the fantastical, the stark and the stylized, designs also paid tribute to contemporary society. The age was depicted as one of liberated, active and healthy living — populated by lithe swimmers, energetic tennis players and daring drivers.

As Art Deco spread in popularity across the world after 1925, it developed a diverse range of local variants. Art Deco had always drawn on a wide range of artistic traditions, but in addition, its distinctive iconography could easily be adapted to suit different national tastes. 'Indo-Deco' from India, for example, came to look quite different from Latin American or North American Deco. But wherever it went, Art Deco was equated with the 'now' of a rapidly changing world. It has proved enduringly popular and, even now, keeps pace with modernity.

The designs in this book are all from the V&A's collections and have been selected to reflect the innovation and variety of Art Deco. You may wish to follow the original colour schemes or experiment with new colourways. The originals can be viewed in the galleries and study rooms of the V&A and online at www.vam.ac.uk.

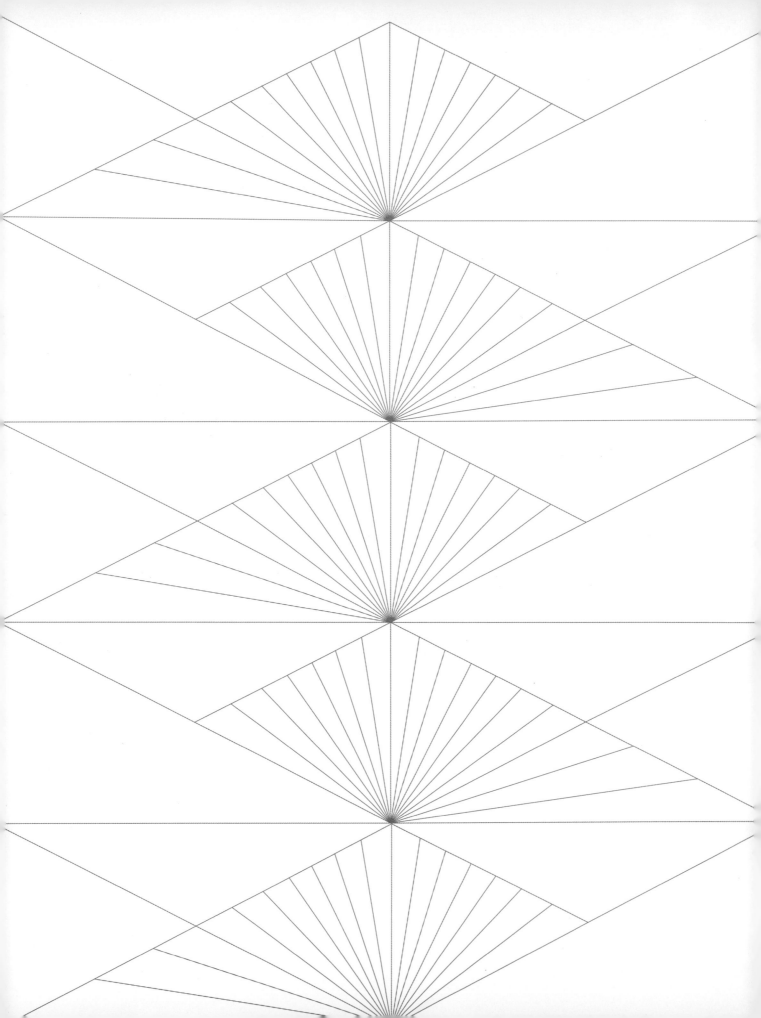

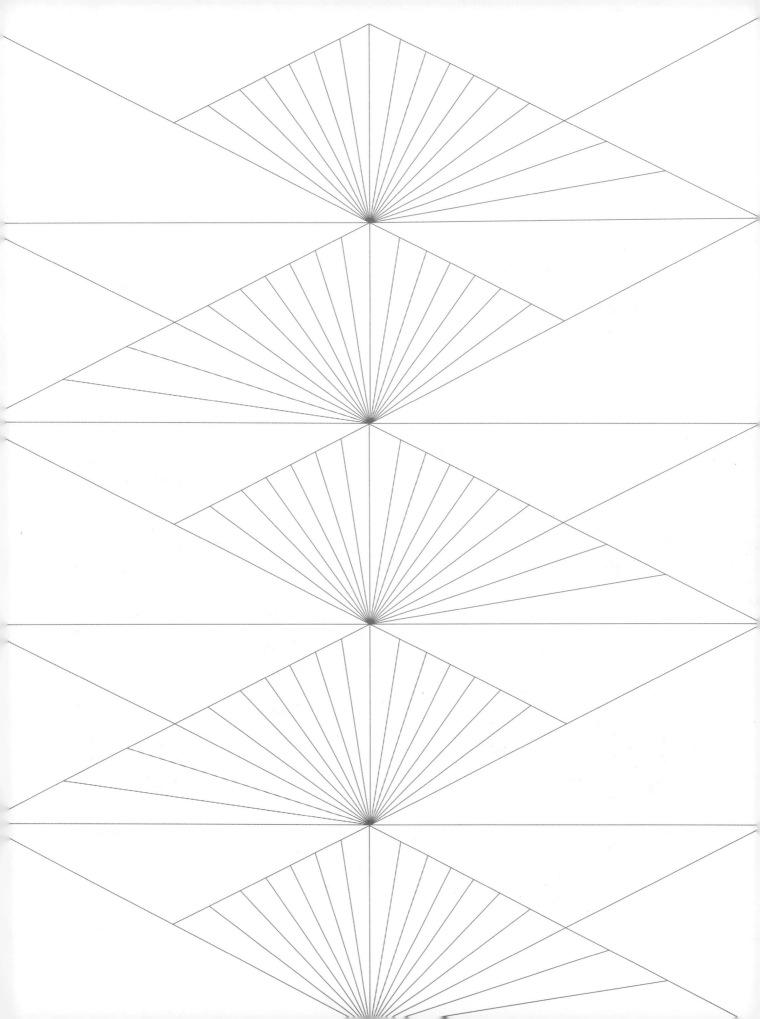

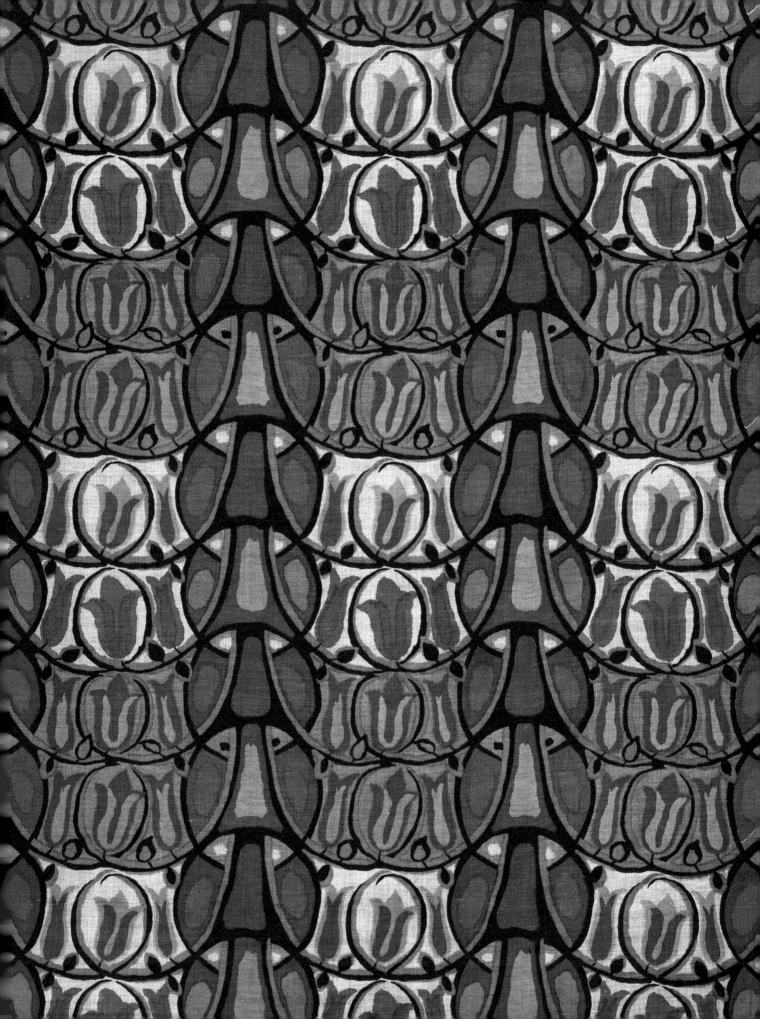

GEORGE BARBIER 1921

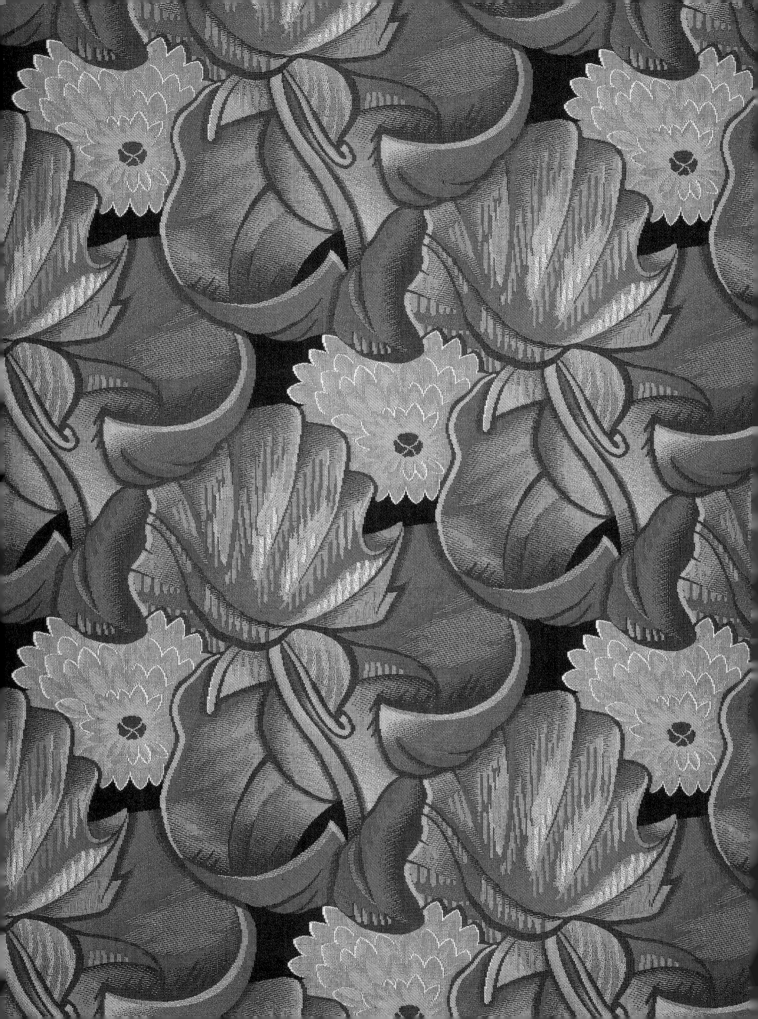

CAPTIONS

'Sunrise' furnishing fabric by Lucienne
Day (1917—2010) for Heal's Fabrics.
Roller-printed cotton. UK, 1969.
Image © Victoria and Albert Museum,
London. Design © Robin and
Lucienne Day Foundation.
V&A: CIRC.39—1969.

Furnishing fabric,
Arthur Sanderson & Sons.
Roller-printed cotton. England, 1930.
© Sanderson
V&A: CIRC.505—1966

Plate 9 'Sheherazade' by Georges
Barbier (1882—1932), from *Modes
et Manières d'Aujourd'hui*.
Print. Paris, France, about 1914.
V&A National Art Library: 95.JJ.22

Plate 3 'Oui!' by Georges Barbier
(1882—1932), from *Falbalas
et Fanfreluches*.
Hand-coloured process engraving.
Paris, France, 1922.
V&A National Art Library: RC.AA.10

Plate 7 'La Parelle' by Georges
Barbier (1882—1932), from
Falbalas et Fanfreluches.
Print. Paris, France, 1925.
V&A National Art Library: RC.AA.10

'Les Fureurs du Tango' by Georges
Barbier (1882—1932), from
La Guirlande des mois Almanach.
Print. Paris, France, about 1917—21.
V&A National Art Library: 95.JJ.19

Furnishing fabric by Minnie McLeish
(1876—1957) for William Foxton Ltd.
Roller-printed cotton. London,
England, 1924.
V&A: T.413—1934.

Furnishing fabric by Gregory Brown
(1887—1941) for William Foxton Ltd.
Block-printed linen. England, 1922.
V&A: T.325—1934

Plate 3 'Le Jugement de Paris' by
Georges Barbier (1882—1932),
from *Falbalas et Fanfreluches*.
Print. Paris, France, 1924.
V&A: E.642—1954

Cover for *Art, Goût, Beauté: Feuillets
d'Elégance Feminine* No. 53,
published by Éditions D'Art.
Print. Paris, France, 1925.
V&A National Art Library: 95.SS.15—17

Furnishing fabric by Pierre Chareau
(1883—1950).
Block-printed linen. France, 1927—28.
V&A: MISC.2:34—1934

Fashion plate depicting two mantles,
from *Art, Goût, Beauté: Feuillets
d'Élégance Feminine*, English edition
published by Éditions d' Art.
Print. Paris, France, 1920s.
V&A National Art Library: 95.SS.15

Plate 48 'Espérez, Robe du Soir de
Worth' by Georges Barbier (1882—1932),
from *Gazette du Bon Ton*, No. 6.
Print. Paris, France, 1922.
V&A National Art Library: 42.NN.1—14

'L'Afrique' furnishing fabric by Robert
Bonfils (1886—1971) for Bianchini-Férier.
Woven silk. Lyons, France, 1925—28.
© Bianchini-Férier
V&A: CIRC.170-1932

'A Game of Tennis' dress fabric by
Helen Wills for Stehli Silks Corporation.
Printed silk crêpe de chine.
New York, USA.
V&A: T.87F—1930

'L' Eau' by Georges Barbier (1882—1932),
from *Falbalas et Fanfreluches*.
Hand-coloured process engraving.
Paris, France, 1925.
V&A: E.630—1954

'L' Oiseau Volage' by Georges Barbier
(1882—1932), from *Modes et Manières
d' Aujourd'hui*.
Print. Paris, France, about 1914.
V&A National Art Library: 95.JJ.22

'Grands Feuillages' by Raoul Dufy
(1877—1953) for Bianchini-Férier.
Block-printed linen. France, about 1920.
© Bianchini-Férier
V&A: MISC.2:30—1934

(Detail) Jewelled vanity case by
Lacloche Frères.
Gold, with black-stained jadeite
and black-backed chalcedony; the lid
set with rose- and brilliant-cut diamonds,
lapis lazuli, turquoise, malachite,
rhodonite, mother-of-pearl and pearl.
Paris, France, about 1926.
V&A: M.24—1976

Fashion plate depicting a chat at a
dinner party, from *Art, Goût, Beauté:
Feuillets d' Élégance Feminine*, English
Edition published by Éditions d'Art.
Print. Paris, France, 1920s.
V&A National Art Library: 95.SS.14—18

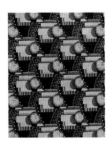

Furnishing fabric, unknown designer.
Cotton plush. France (probably),
1925—30.
V&A: T.120-1980

'Un Peu', depicting a House of Worth
outfit, by Georges Barbier (1882—1932),
from *Gazette du Bon Ton*.
Print. Paris, France, 1913.
V&A National Art Library: 42. NN.1—14

(Detail) 'La Folie du Jour' by Georges
Barbier (1882—1932), from *Journal des
Dames et des Modes*, published by Aux
Bureaux du Journal des Dames.
Paris, France, 1914. V&A National Art
Library: 42.NN.25

Furnishing fabric by Gregory Brown
(1887—1941) for William Foxton Ltd.
Block-printed linen. England, 1922.
V&A: T.307—1934

Fashion plate depicting À la Reine
d'Angleterre and A. Wilmarts designs,
from *Art, Goût, Beauté: Feuillets
d'Élégance Feminine*, English Edition
published by Éditions d' Art.
Print. Paris, France, 1920s.
V&A National Art Library: 95.SS.15

Plate 9 'Deux Heures du Matin,
Manteaux du Worth' by Georges Barbier
(1882—1932), from *Gazette du Bon Ton*.
Hand-coloured process engraving.
Paris, France, 1923.
V&A National Art Library: 95.SS.14—18

(Detail) Cigarette case
by Gérard Sandoz.
Enamelled silver, lacquer and eggshell.
Paris, France, about 1929.
V&A: CIRC.329—1972

(Detail) Vase, Ando Company.
Cloisonné enamel. Nagoya, Japan,
about 1930—50.
V&A: FE:52:1—2011

(Detail) Vase by René Buthaud.
Stoneware with crackled glaze, painted
in enamels and lustre. Bordeaux, France,
about 1928—1930.
V&A: C.292—1987

(Detail) Vase and cover by Henri
Rapin (1873—1939) & Anne
Marie Fontaine (?—1938).
Porcelain. Sèvres, France,
about 1925—33.
V&A: C.116:1-1992

Furnishing fabric, F. W. Grafton & Co.
Roller-printed cotton.
Manchester, England, 1921.
V&A: T.442—1934

'Surfers' dress fabric,
Calico Printers Association.
Roller-printed cotton. Manchester,
England. 1937.
V&A: T.264—1987

'La Belle Personne' by Georges Barbier
(1882—1932), from Le Pavillon de
l' Élégance: L' Exposition Des Arts
Decoratifs et Industriels Modernes,
from *Gazette du Bon Ton*.
Print. Paris, France, 1925.
V&A National Art Library: 512.B.94

'La Terre' by Georges Barbier
(1882—1932), from *Falbalas
et Fanfreluches*.
Hand-coloured process engraving.
Paris, France, 1925.
V&A: E.627—1954

'Mandalay' furnishing fabric
by Felix C. Gotto for Old Bleach
Linen Company Ltd.
Linen. Northern Ireland, about 1935.
V&A: CIRC.223—935

Furnishing fabric by George Sheringham
(1884—1937) for Tootal, Broadhurst,
Lee & Co.
Roller-printed cotton.
Manchester, England, about 1925.
V&A: CIRC.475—1966

'Des Roses dans La Nuit'
by Georges Barbier (1882—1932),
from *Gazette du Bon Ton*.
Print. Paris, France, 1922.
V&A National Art Library: 42. NN.1—14

'From Harwich through Holland
for the Continent' poster
by Claude Flight (1881—1955) for
London and North Eastern Railway.
Colour lithograph. England, about 1929.
V&A: E.1476—1929

Door surround by Raymond Hood
(1881—1934) for the Birmingham
Guild of Handicraft.
Enamel on bronze. Birmingham, England.
V&A: M.75:1 to 14—1982

Furnishing fabric,
Arthur Sanderson & Sons Ltd.
Roller-printed cotton. England, c.1920s.
© Sanderson
V&A: CIRC.623—1964

'Voici mes ailes!' by Georges Barbier
(1882—1932), from *Falbalas*
et Fanfreluches.
Hand-coloured process engraving.
Paris, France, 1922.
V&A: E.620—1954

Bodice of a dress, detail
of repeat, by Wiener Werkstätte.
Block-printed silk.
Austria, about 1910—20.
V&A: T.855—2000

Fan depicting a woman with vines,
leaves and grapes by Georges
Barbier (1882—1932) for
Madame Paquin (1839—1936).
Paper and silk. Paris, France, 1911.
V&A: T.333-1978

Plate 66 'Sortileges, Robe du Soir
de Beer' by Georges Barbier
(1882—1932), from *Gazette du Bon Ton*.
V&A National Art Library: 42.NN.1—14

MORE READING ON ART DECO:

Alastair Duncan, *Art Deco Sculpture*, Thames & Hudson, 2016

Rodney and Diana Capstick-Dale, *Art Deco Collectibles:
Fashionable Objets from the Jazz Age,* Thames & Hudson,
2016

Alastair Duncan, *Art Deco Complete: The Definitive
Guide to the Decorative Arts of the 1920s and 30s,*
Thames & Hudson, 2009

Ghislaine Wood, *Essential Art Deco,* V&A Publishing, 2003

Charlotte Benton, Tim Benton and Ghislaine Wood (eds.)
Art Deco 1910—39, V&A Publishing, 2003